Thomas Jefferson

HIS ESSENTIAL WISDOM

Thomas Jefferson

HIS ESSENTIAL WISDOM

Edited by

Carol Kelly-Gangi

FALL RIVER PRESS

To John, John Christopher, and Emily Grace with love.

Compilation © 2010 by Carol Kelly-Gangi

Book design by Maria Mann

Fall River Press
122 Fifth Avenue
New York, NY 10011

ISBN: 978-1-4351-2312-0

Printed and bound in the United States of America

1 3 5 7 9 10 8 6 4 2

Contents

INTRODUCTION

Here was buried
Thomas Jefferson
Author of the Declaration of American Independence
of the Statute of Virginia for religious freedom
and Father of the University of Virginia.

In reading the epitaph that Thomas Jefferson wrote for his tombstone, it seems incredible that he chose to omit that he had been elected and served as the president of the United States for two terms. That Jefferson is a figure full of contradiction and paradox has been well documented. He was a man who professed throughout his life that he wanted nothing more than to retire and return to his life of family and farming at Monticello, yet he served the public for forty years as a member of Congress, governor, ambassador, secretary of state, vice president, and two-time president. He was a tireless advocate for the rights of small government, but as president, he more than doubled the size of the United States. And as the drafter of the Declaration of Independence, he boldly proclaimed that all men were created equal with the God-given rights of life, liberty, and the pursuit of happiness, while he himself was a lifelong slave-holder with deeply held views of racial inequalities. Adding yet another layer of complexity to our reckoning of Jefferson is the fact that though he was a vigorous opponent of the so-called "mixing of races," both scientific and circumstantial evidence today indicates that Jefferson in all likelihood fathered one or more children with his slave Sally Hemmings. Still, his supreme place in American history and for people everywhere who champion the right to self-government, is unequalled. In the more than 180 years since his death, his words continue to resonate as the blueprint for the ideals of American democracy.

Thomas Jefferson: His Essential Wisdom gathers together more than three hundred quotations from Thomas Jefferson drawn from his public papers, addresses, essays, his one book, *Notes on the State of Virginia,* and from his voluminous personal correspondence—of which he was eminently proud and which amounted to more than 18,000 letters over the course of his lifetime.

This selection of Jefferson's thoughts and insights provides a glimpse into his philosophical, intellectual, literary, and political genius. Never willing to just submit to another's "creed" on any subject where he could think and reason for himself, Jefferson's philosophies can rather be gleaned from a perusal of the treasure that are his writings, and, of course, from his life as he lived it. The quotations themselves are arranged thematically and represent the subjects of greatest import to Jefferson and the other Founding Fathers. In these excerpts, Jefferson speaks fervently about the natural rights, freedom, equality, justice, and Democracy, that were the underpinnings of the great American experiment upon which he and his fellow revolutionaries were embarking. Elsewhere, Jefferson offers his views on the role of government; the value of religion; the need for morality; and the snares of politics. He reveals his struggles with the issue of slavery and race—representing what one historian has called the core contradiction of his life. Here as well can be found practical extracts of Jefferson's wisdom on such varied subjects as marital happiness, exercise, time management, and the benefits of civility. And in perhaps the most poignant section of the book, Jefferson expresses the inestimable pleasures of home, family, and friendship, and in the process reveals himself as a loving husband, doting father and grandfather, and devoted friend.

Thomas Jefferson: His Essential Wisdom invites readers to once again consider the man who has been called "The Apostle of Americanism," who perhaps more than anyone else in our history personified the spirit of enlightened and revolutionary ideas that formed the basis of the American experiment, and whose oath against "every form of tyranny over the mind of man," still ennobles and challenges us today.

—Carol Kelly-Gangi
Rumson, New Jersey, 2010

EARLY YEARS

I had the good fortune to become acquainted very early with some characters of very high standing, and to feel the incessant wish that I could even become what they were.

—Jefferson's *Autobiography*

It was my great good fortune, and what probably fixed the destinies of my life, that Dr. William Small of Scotland was the professor of mathematics, a man profound in most of the useful branches of science, with a happy talent of communication, correct and gentlemanly manners, and an enlarged and liberal mind. He, most happily for me, became soon attached to me, and made me his daily companion when not engaged in the school, and from his conversation I got my first views of the expansion of science, and of the system of things in which we are placed.

—Jefferson's *Autobiography*

All things here appear to me to trudge on in one and the same round: we rise in the morning that we may eat breakfast, dinner and supper, and we go to bed again that we may get up the next morning and go the same, so that you never saw two peas more alike than our yesterday and today.

—Letter to John Page, January 20, 1763, where Jefferson expresses
the monotony of his visits home from William and Mary

From the circumstances of my position, I was often thrown into the society of horse-racers, card-players, fox-hunters, scientific and professional men, and of dignified men; and many a time have I asked myself, in the enthusiastic moment of the death of a fox, the victory of a favorite horse, the issue of a question eloquently argued at the bar, or in the great council of the nation, well, which of these kinds of reputation should I prefer? That of a horse-jockey, a fox-hunter, an orator, or the honest advocate of my country's rights?

—Letter to Thomas Jefferson Randolph, November 24, 1808,
where Jefferson recalls his early days at William and Mary

I do not like the ups and downs of a country life: today you are frolicking with a fine girl, and tomorrow you are moping by yourself. Thanks God! I shall shortly be where my happiness will be less interrupted.

—Letter to John Page, January 19, 1764

Search the Herald's office for the arms of my family. I have what
I have been told were the family arms, but on what authority I
know not. It is possible there may be none. If so, I would with your
assistance become a purchaser, having Sterne's word for it that a
coat of arms may be purchased as cheap as any other coat.

—Letter to Thomas Adams, February 20, 1771

When the famous Resolutions of 1765, against the Stamp-act, were
proposed, I was yet a student of law in Williamsburg. I attended
the debate however at the door of the lobby of the H. of Burgesses,
& heard the splendid display of Mr. Henry's talents as a popular
orator. They were great indeed; such as I have never heard from any
other man. He appeared to me to speak as Homer wrote.

—Jefferson's *Autobiography*

FOUNDING FATHER

Can any one reason be assigned why 160,000 electors in the island of Great Britain should give law to four millions in the States of America, every individual of whom is equal to every individual of them in virtue, in understanding, and in bodily strength? Were this to be admitted, instead of being a free people, as we have hitherto supposed, and mean to continue ourselves, we should suddenly be found the slaves not of one but of 160,000 tyrants.

But can his majesty . . . put down all law under his feet? Can he erect a power superior to that which erected himself? He has done it indeed by force, but let him remember that force cannot give right. . . . The God who gave us life gave us liberty at the same time: the hand of force may destroy, but cannot disjoin them. This, sire, is our last, our determined resolution.

—A Summary View of the Rights of British America, 1774

Our cause is just. Our union is perfect. Our internal resources are great, and, if necessary, foreign assistance is undoubtedly attainable. We gratefully acknowledge, as signal instances of the Divine favour towards us, that his Providence would not permit us to be called into this severe controversy, until we were grown up to our present strength, had been previously exercised in warlike operation, and possessed of the means of defending ourselves. With hearts fortified with these animating reflections, we most solemnly, before God and the world, declare, that, exerting the utmost energy of those powers, which our beneficent Creator hath graciously bestowed upon us, the arms we have been compelled by our enemies to assume, we will, in defiance of every hazard, with unabating firmness and perseverence, employ for the preservation of our liberties; being with one mind resolved to die freemen rather than to live slaves.

—Declaration of the Causes and Necessity of Taking Up Arms, 1775. This first draft by Jefferson was considered too militant by the Continental Congress. A second draft was written by John Dickinson, and the final was a combination from the work of both men.

The committee for drawing the Declaration of Independence desired me to do it. It was accordingly done.

—Jefferson's *Autobiography*

Within this week we have received the unhappy news of an action of considerable magnitude, between the King's troops and our brethren of Boston, in which it is said five hundred of the former, with the Earl of Percy, are slain... This accident has cut off our last hope of reconciliation, and a frenzy of revenge seems to have seized all ranks of people.

—Letter to William Small, May 7, 1775

May it be to the world, what I believe it will be, (to some parts
sooner, to others later, but finally to all), the signal of arousing
men to burst the chains under which monkish ignorance and
superstition had persuaded them to bind themselves, and to assume
the blessings and security of self-government.

—Letter to Roger C. Weightman, June 24, 1826, referring
to the decision for Independence made in 1776

Reason first: You are a Virginian and a Virginian ought to appear at
the head of this business. Reason second: I am obnoxious, suspected
and unpopular. You are very much otherwise. Reason third: You can
write ten times better than I can.

—John Adams to Thomas Jefferson on why the latter was the better
choice to draft The Declaration of Independence, June 1776

When, in the course of human events, it becomes necessary for
one people to dissolve the political bands which have connected
them with another, and to assume among the powers of the earth
the separate and equal station to which the laws of nature and
of nature's God entitle them, a decent respect to the opinions of
mankind requires that they should declare the causes which impel
them to the separation.

We hold these truths to be self evident: that all men are created
equal; that they are endowed by their Creator with inherent and
inalienable Rights; that among these, are Life, Liberty, and the

pursuit of Happiness; that to secure these rights, Governments are instituted among Men, deriving their just powers from the consent of the governed; that whenever any Form of Government becomes destructive of these ends, it is the Right of the people to alter or abolish it, and to institute new Government, laying its foundation on such principles, and organizing its powers in such form, as to them shall seem most likely to effect their Safety and Happiness.

—The Declaration of Independence, July 4, 1776

Prudence . . . will dictate that Governments long established should not be changed for light and transient causes; and accordingly all experience hath shewn that mankind are more disposed to suffer, while evils are sufferable than to right themselves by abolishing the forms to which they are accustomed. But when a long train of abuses and usurpations, pursuing invariably the same Object evinces a design to reduce them under absolute Despotism, it is their right, it is their duty, to throw off such Government, and to provide new Guards for their future security.

—The Declaration of Independence, July 4, 1776

And for the support of this declaration, we mutually pledge to each other our lives, our fortunes, and our sacred honour.

—Closing words of The Declaration of Independence, July 4, 1776

This was the object of the Declaration of Independence. Not to find out new principles, or new arguments, never before thought of, not merely to say things which had never been said before; but to place before mankind the common sense of the subject; i[n] terms so plain and firm as to command their assent, and to justify ourselves in the independent stand we [are c]ompelled to take.

—Letter to Henry Lee, May 8, 1825

The first question was whether we should propose to abolish the whole existing system of laws and prepare a new and complete institute, or preserve the general system and only modify it to the present state of things.

—Jefferson, from his *Autobiography*, recalling the business at hand for the new House of Delegates in 1776

The abolition of primogeniture, and equal partition of inheritances, removed the feudal and unnatural distinctions which made one member of every family rich, and all the rest poor, substituting equal partition, the best of all Agrarian laws.

—Jefferson's *Autobiography*

The affection of my countrymen...was the only reward I ever asked or could have felt.

—Letter to James Monroe, 1782

The memory of the American Revolution will be immortal, and will immortalize those who record it. The reward is encouraging, and will justify all those pains which a rigorous investigation of facts will render necessary.

—Letter to Hilliard D'Auberteuil, 1786

I have no fear, but that the result of our experiment will be, that men may be trusted to govern themselves without a master. Could the contrary of this be proved, I should conclude, either that there is no God, or that he is a malevolent being.

—Letter to David Hartley, 1787

It is part of the American character to consider nothing as desperate, to surmount every difficulty by resolution and contrivance.

—Letter to Martha Jefferson, March 28, 1787

If there be one principle more deeply rooted than any other in the mind of every American, it is, that we should have nothing to do with conquest.

—Letter to William Short, 1791

We confide in our strength, without boasting of it; we respect that of others, without fearing it.

—Letter to William Carmichael and William Short, 1793

I like the dreams of the future better than the history of the past.

—Letter to John Adams, August 1, 1816

I am a sect by myself, as far as I know.

—Letter to Ezra Stiles, June 25, 1819

And even should the cloud of barbarism and despotism again obscure the science and libraries of Europe, this country remains to preserve and restore light and liberty to them. In short, the flames kindled on the fourth of July, 1776, have spread over too much of the globe to be extinguished by the feeble engines of despotism; on the contrary, they will consume these engines and all who work them.

—Letter to John Adams, September 12, 1821

The example we have given to the world is single, that of changing the form of our government under the authority of reason only, without bloodshed.

—Letter to Ralph Izar, 1788

I join you cordially, and await [God's] time and will with more readiness than reluctance. May we meet there again, in Congress, with our ancient Colleagues, and receive them with the seal of approbation, 'Well done, good and faithful servants.'

—Letter to John Adams, April 11, 1823, written two days before Jefferson's eightieth birthday

GOVERNMENT
AND DEMOCRACY

The whole art of government consists in the art of being honest.

—A Summary View of the Rights of British America, 1774

It is error alone which needs the support of government. Truth can stand by itself.

—Notes on the State of Virginia, 1782

Governments are instituted among men, deriving their just powers from the consent of the governed.

—The Declaration of Independence, July 4, 1776

The spirit of resistance to government is so valuable on certain occasions that I wish it to be always kept alive. It will often be exercised when wrong, but better so than not to be exercised at all.

—Letter to Abigail Adams, February 2, 1787

The republican is the only form of government which is not eternally at open or secret war with the rights of mankind.

—Letter to William Hunter, 1790

There is no king, who, with a sufficient force, is not always ready to make himself absolute.

—Letter to George Wythe, August 13, 1786

I know, indeed, that some honest men fear that a republican government cannot be strong; that this government is not strong enough. But would the honest patriot, in the full tide of successful experiment, abandon a government which has so far kept us free and firm, on the theoretic and visionary fear that this government, the world's best hope, may by possibility want energy to preserve itself?

I trust not. I believe this, on the contrary, the strongest government on earth. I believe it is the only one where every man, at the call of the laws, would fly to the standard of the law, and would meet invasions of the public order as his own personal concern.

—First Inaugural Address, 1801

The execution of the laws is more important than the making of them.

—Letter to the Abbé Arnoux, 1789

The government is the strongest of which every man feels himself a part.

—Letter to H. D. Tiffin, February 2, 1807

I am not among those who fear the people. They, and not the rich, are our dependence for continued freedom.

—Letter to Samuel Kercheval, July 12, 1816

I sincerely wish you may find it convenient to come here. The pleasure of the trip will be less than you expect but the utility greater. It will make you adore your own country, its soil, its climate, its equality, liberty, laws, people & manners. My God! How little do my country men know what precious blessings they are in possession of, and which no other people on earth enjoy.

I confess I had no idea of it myself. While we shall see multiplied instances of Europeans going to live in America, I will venture to say no man now living will ever see an instance of an American removing to settle in Europe & continuing there.

—Letter to James Monroe, 1785, while serving as Minister to France

I find the general fate of humanity here most deplorable. The truth of Voltaire's observation, offers itself perpetually, that every man here must be either the hammer or the anvil.

—Letter to Charles Bellini, 1785

Among [European governments], under pretense of governing, they have divided their nations into two classes, wolves and sheep.

—Letter to Edward Carrington, 1787

When we get piled upon one another in large cities, as in Europe, we shall become corrupt as in Europe.

—Letter to James Madison, December 20, 1787

Our laws, language, religion, politics, & manners are so deeply laid in English foundations, that we shall never cease to consider their history as a part of ours, and to study ours in that as it's origin.

—Letter to William Duane, 1810

I agree with you that there is a natural aristocracy among men. The grounds of this are virtue and talents. . . . There is also an artificial aristocracy founded on wealth and birth, without either virtue or talents. . . . The artificial aristocracy is a mischievous ingredient in government, and provision should be made to prevent its ascendancy.

—Letter to John Adams, October 28, 1813

A wise and frugal Government, which shall restrain men from injuring one another, shall leave them otherwise free to regulate their own pursuits of industry and improvement, and shall not take from the mouth of labor the bread it has earned. This is the sum of good government.

—First Inaugural Address, March 4, 1801

His mind was really powerful, but chained by native partialities to everything English. He had formed exaggerated ideas of the superior perfection of the English constitution, the superior wisdom of their government, and sincerely believed it for the good of this country to make them its model in everything; without considering that what might be wise and good for a nation essentially commercial, and entangled in complicated intercourse with numerous and powerful neighbors, might not be so for one essentially agricultural, and insulated by nature from the abusive governments of the old world.

—Letter to William H. Crawford, 1816, writing about Alexander Hamilton

I know no safe depository of the ultimate powers of society but the people themselves; and if we think them not enlightened enough to exercise their control with a wholesome discretion, the remedy is not to take it from them, but to inform their discretion by education.

—Letter to W. C. Jarvis, September 28, 1820

My idea is that the Federal government should be organized into legislative, executive, and judiciary, as are the State governments, and some peaceable means of enforcement devised for the Federal head over the States.

—Letter to J. Blair, 1787

Agriculture, manufactures, commerce, and navigation, the four pillars of our prosperity, are the most thriving when left to individual enterprise.

—First Annual Message to Congress, December 8, 1801

The idea of creating a national bank I do not concur in, because it seems now decided that Congress has not that power (although I sincerely wish they had it exclusively), and because I think there is already a vast redundancy rather than a scarcity of paper medium.

—Letter to Thomas Law, 1813

The Constitution . . . meant that its coordinate branches should be checks on each other. But the opinion which gives to the judges the right to decide what laws are constitutional and what not, not only for themselves in their own sphere of action but for the Legislature and Executive also in their spheres, would make the Judiciary a despotic branch.

—Letter to Abigail Adams, 1804

Everything predicted by the enemies of banks, in the beginning, is now coming to pass. We are to be ruined now by the deluge of bank paper. It is cruel that such revolutions in private fortunes should be at the mercy of avaricious adventurers, who, instead of employing their capital, if any they have, in manufactures, commerce, and other useful pursuits, make it an instrument to burden all the interchanges of property with their swindling profits, profits which are the price of no useful industry of theirs.

—Letter to Thomas Cooper, 1814

I am an enemy to all banks discounting bills or notes for anything but coin.

—Letter to Thomas Cooper, 1814

Some men look at constitutions with sanctimonious reverence, and deem them like the ark of the covenant, too sacred to be touched. They ascribe to the men of the preceding age a wisdom more than human, and suppose what they did to be beyond amendment....
I am certainly not an advocate for frequent and untried changes in laws and constitutions. I think moderate imperfections had better be borne with; because, when once known, we accommodate ourselves to them, and find practical means of correcting their ill effects. But I know also that laws and institutions must go hand in hand with the progress of the human mind. As that becomes more developed, more enlightened, as new discoveries are made, new

truths disclosed, and manners and opinions change with the change of circumstances, institution must advance also, and keep pace with the times. We might as well require a man to wear still the coat which fitted him when a boy, as civilized society to remain ever under the regimen of their barbarous ancestors.

—Letter to Samuel Kercheval, July 12, 1816

We may say with truth and meaning that governments are more or less republican, as they have more or less of the element of popular election and control in their composition; and believing, as I do, that the mass of the citizens is the safest depository of their own rights, and especially, that the evils flowing from the duperies of the people are less injurious than those from the egoism of their agents, I am a friend to that composition of government which has in it the most of this ingredient. And I sincerely believe, with you, that banking establishments are more dangerous than standing armies; and that the principle of spending money to be paid by posterity, under the name of funding, is but swindling futurity on a large scale.

—Letter to John Taylor, 1816

The Constitution is a mere thing of wax in the hands of the judiciary, which they may twist and shape into any form they please.

—Letter to Judge Spencer Roane, 1819

On every question of construction, carry ourselves back to the time when the Constitution was adopted, recollect the spirit manifested in the debates, and instead of trying what meaning may be squeezed out of the text, or invented against it, conform to the probable one in which it was passed.

—Letter to Justice William Johnson, 1823

I have a right to nothing which another has a right to take away. And Congress will have a right to take away trial by jury in all civil cases. Let me add that a bill of rights is what the people are entitled to against every government on earth, general or particular, and what no just government should refuse or rest on inference.

—Letter to James Madison, December 20, 1787

I never will, by any word or act, bow to the shrine of intolerance, or admit a right of inquiry into the religious opinions of others. On the contrary, we are bound, you, I, and everyone, to make common cause, even with error itself, to maintain the common right of freedom of conscience.

—Letter to Edward Dowse, 1803

No government ought to be without censors; and where the press is free, no [government] ever will.

—Letter to George Washington, September 9, 1792

The office of reformer of the superstitions of a nation is ever dangerous.

—Letter to William Short, 1820

I am for... freedom of the press and against all violations of the Constitution to silence by force, and not by reason, the complaints or criticisms, just or unjust, of our citizens against the conduct of their agents.

—Letter to Elbridge Gerry, 1799

Error of opinion may be tolerated where reason is left free to combat it.

—First Inaugural Address, 1801

Subject opinion to coercion: whom will you make your inquisitors? Fallible men; men governed by bad passions, by private as well as public reasons. And why subject it to coercion? To produce uniformity. But is uniformity of opinion desirable? No more than of face and stature.

—Virginia Act for Religious Freedom, 1786

To the press alone, chequered as it is with abuses, the world is
indebted for all the triumphs which have been gained by reason
and humanity over error and oppression. . . .

—Virginia and Kentucky Resolutions, 1799

History I believe furnishes no example of a priest-ridden people
maintaining a free civil government. This marks the lowest grade
of ignorance, of which their political as well as religious leaders
will always avail themselves for their own purpose.

—Letter to Baron von Humboldt, 1813

I think myself that we have more machinery of government than is
necessary, too many parasites living on the labor of the industrious.

—Letter to William Ludlow, 1824

With all the imperfections of our present government, it is without
comparison the best existing, or that ever did exist.

—Letter to Edward Carrington, 1787

FREEDOM AND RIGHTS

Almighty God hath created the mind free. All attempts to influence it by temporal punishments or burdens... are a departure from the plan of the Holy Author of our religion... No man shall be compelled to frequent or support any religious worship or ministry or shall otherwise suffer on account of his religious opinions or belief, but all men shall be free to profess and by argument to maintain, their opinions in matters of religion. I know but one code of morality for men whether acting singly or collectively.

—Inscription on The Jefferson Memorial from
The Virginia Act for Religious Freedom, 1786

God forbid we should ever be twenty years without such a rebellion. The people cannot be all, and always, well informed. The part which is wrong will be discontented, in proportion to the importance of the facts they misconceive. If they remain quiet under such misconceptions, it is lethargy, the forerunner of death to the public liberty. . . . What country before ever existed a century and half without a rebellion? And what country can preserve its liberties if their rulers are not warned from time to time that their people preserve the spirit of resistance? Let them take arms. The remedy is to set them right as to facts, pardon and pacify them. What signify a few lives lost in a century or two? The tree of liberty must be refreshed from time to time with the blood of patriots and tyrants.

It is its natural manure.

—Letter to William S. Smith, November 13, 1787

We are not to expect to be translated from despotism to liberty in a featherbed.

—Letter to the Marquis de Lafayette, April 2, 1790

I continue eternally attached to the principles of your Revolution. I hope it will end in the establishment of some firm government, friendly to liberty, and capable of maintaining it. If it does, the world will become inevitably free.

—Letter to J. P. Brissot de Warville, 1793, commenting on the French Revolution

Resolved . . . that it would be a dangerous delusion were a confidence in the men of our choice to silence our fears for the safety of our rights: that confidence is everywhere the parent of despotism—free government is founded in jealousy, and not in confidence. . . .

—The Kentucky Resolutions, October 1798

The most important bill in our whole code is that for the diffusion of knowledge among the people. No other sure foundation can be devised, for the preservation of freedom and happiness.

—Letter to George Wythe, 1786

The people are the only sure reliance for the preservation of our liberty.

—Letter to James Madison, 1787

The natural progress of things is for liberty to yield and government to gain ground.

—Letter to Colonel Edward Carrington, 1788

Our liberty depends on the freedom of the press, and that cannot be limited without being lost.

—Letter to James Currie, 1786

Whenever the people are well informed, they can be trusted with their own government; that whenever things get so far wrong as to attract their notice, they may be relied on to set them to rights.

—Letter to Richard Price, January 8, 1789

The basis of our government being the opinion of the people, the very first object should be to keep that right; and were it left to me to decide whether we should have a government without newspapers, or newspapers without a government, I should not hesitate a moment to prefer the latter.

—Letter to Edward Carrington, January 16, 1787

For God's sake, let us freely hear both sides!

—Letter to Nicholas G. Dufief, April 19, 1814

To preserve the freedom of the human mind then and freedom of the press, every spirit should be ready to devote itself to martyrdom; for as long as we may think as we will, and speak as we think, the condition of man will proceed in improvement.

—Letter to William Green Mumford, June 18, 1799

It behooves every man who values liberty of conscience for himself, to resist invasions of it in the case others.

—Letter to Benjamin Rush, April 21, 1803

Nothing . . . is unchangeable but the inherent and inalienable rights of man.

—Letter to John Cartwright, June 5, 1824

What is true of every member of the society individually, is true of them all collectively, since the rights of the whole can be no more than the sum of the rights of the individuals.

—Letter to James Madison, September 6, 1789

Our legislators are not sufficiently apprized of the rightful limits of their power; that their true office is to declare and enforce only our natural rights . . . and to take none of them from us. No man has a natural right to commit aggression on the equal rights of another; and this is all from which the laws ought to restrain him . . . and the idea is quite unfounded, that on entering into society we give up any natural right.

—Letter to Francis W. Gilmer, June 27, 1816

I have sworn upon the altar of God, eternal hostility against every form of tyranny over the mind of man.

—Letter to Benjamin Rush, September 23, 1800

EQUALITY, LAW, AND JUSTICE

All men are created equal.

—The Declaration of Independence, July 4, 1776

We must await with patience the workings of an overruling Providence, and hope that that is preparing the deliverance of these, our suffering brethren.

—Letter to M. de Meunier, 1786, writing about slavery.

The whole commerce between master and slave is a perpetual exercise of the most boisterous passions, the most unremitting despotism on the one part, and degrading submissions on the other. Our children see this, and learn to imitate it; for man is an imitative animal . . . The parent storms, the child looks on, catches the lineaments of wrath, puts on the same airs in the circle of smaller slaves, gives a loose to the worst of his passions, and thus nursed, educated, and daily exercised in tyranny, cannot but be stamped by it with odious peculiarities.

—Notes on the State of Virginia, 1782

Can the liberties of a nation be thought secure when we have removed their only firm basis, a conviction in the minds of the people that these liberties are of the gift of God? That they are not to be violated but with his wrath? Indeed, I tremble for my country when I reflect that God is just; that his justice cannot sleep forever; that considering numbers, nature and natural means only, a revolution of the wheel of fortune, an exchange of situation is among possible events; that it may become probable by supernatural interference! The Almighty has no attribute which can take side with us in such a contest.

—*Notes on the State of Virginia*, 1782, referring to slavery

What a stupendous, what an incomprehensible machine is man! Who can endure toil, famine, stripes, imprisonment and death itself in vindication of his own liberty, and the next moment . . . inflict on his fellow men a bondage, one hour of which is fraught with more misery than ages of that which he rose in rebellion to oppose.

—Letter to Jean Nicholas Demeunier, January 24, 1786

All, too, will bear in mind this sacred principle, that though the will of the majority is in all cases to prevail, that will to be rightful must be reasonable; that the minority possess their equal rights, which equal law must protect, and to violate would be oppression.

—First Inaugural Address, March 4, 1801

I am miserable till I shall owe not a shilling. The moment that shall be the case, I shall feel myself at liberty to do something for the comfort of my slaves.

—Letter to Nicholas Lewis, 1786

I congratulate you, my dear friend, on the law of your state for suspending the importation of slaves . . . this abomination must have an end, and there is a superior bench reserved in heaven for those who hasten it.

—Letter to Edward Rutledge, 1787

I congratulate you on the approach of the period at which you may interpose your authority constitutionally, to withdraw the citizens of the United States from all further participation in those violations of human rights which have been so long continued on the unoffending inhabitants of Africa, and which the morality, the reputation, and the best interests of our country, have long been eager to proscribe. Although no law you may pass can take prohibitory effect till the first day of the year one thousand eight hundred and eight, yet the intervening period is not too long to prevent, by timely notice, expeditions which cannot be completed before that day.

—Sixth Annual Message to Congress, 1806

My opinion has ever been that, until more can be done for them, we should endeavor, with those whom fortune has thrown on our hands, to feed and clothe them well, protect them from ill usage, require such reasonable labor only as is performed voluntarily by freemen, and be led by no repugnances to abdicate them, and our duties to them. The laws do not permit us to turn them loose, if that were for their good; and to commute them for other property is to commit them to those whose usage of them we cannot control.

—Letter to Edward Coles, 1814

The hour of emancipation is advancing . . . this enterprise is for the young; for those who can follow it up, and bear it through to it's consummation. It shall have all my prayers, and these are the only weapons of an old man.

—Letter Letter to Edward Coles, 1814

Bigotry is the disease of ignorance, of morbid minds; enthusiasm of the free and buoyant. Education & free discussion are the antidotes of both.

—Letter to John Adams, August 1, 1816

I had for a long time ceased to read newspapers, or pay any attention to public affairs, confident they were in good hands, and content to be a passenger in our bark to the shore from which

I am not distant. But this momentous question, like a firebell in the night, awakened and filled me with terror. I considered it at once as the knell of the Union.

—Letter to John Holmes, April 22, 1820, referring to the Missouri Compromise

We have the wolf by the ears, and we can neither hold him nor safely let him go. Justice is in one scale, self-preservation in the other.

—Letter to John Holmes, April 22, 1820, referring to slavery

I regret that I am now to die in the belief, that the useless sacrifice of themselves by the generation of 1776, to acquire self-government and happiness to their country, is to be thrown away by the unwise and unworthy passions of their sons, and that my only consolation is to be, that I live not to weep over it. If they would but dispassionately weigh the blessings they will throw away, against an abstract principle more likely to be effected by union than by scission, they would pause before they would perpetrate this act of suicide on themselves, and of treason against the hopes of the world. To yourself, as the faithful advocate of the Union, I tender the offering of my high esteem and respect.

—Letter to John Holmes, April 22, 1820

Nothing is more certainly written in the book of fate, than that these people are to be free; nor is it less certain that the two races, equally free, cannot live in the same government. Nature, habit, opinion have drawn indelible lines of distinction between them.

—Jefferson's *Autobiography*, in notes describing some of the debates of 1779 on slavery

Equal and exact justice to all men . . . freedom of religion, freedom of the press, freedom of the person under the protection of the habeas corpus; and trial by juries impartially selected—these principles form the bright constellation that has gone before us.

—First Inaugural Address, March 4, 1801

You seem to consider the federal judges as the ultimate arbiters of all constitutional questions, a very dangerous doctrine, indeed, and one which would place us under the despotism of an oligarchy. Our judges are as honest as other men, and not more so. They have with others the same passions for the party, for power and the privilege of the corps. Their power is the more dangerous, as they are in office for life and not responsible, as the other functionaries are, to the elective control. The Constitution has erected no such single tribunal, knowing that to whatever hands confided, with the corruptions of time and party, its members would become despots. It has more wisely made all departments co-equal and co-sovereign within themselves.

—Letter to William Charles Jarvis, 1820

It is better to toss up cross and pile [heads or tails] in a cause than to refer it to a judge whose mind is warped by any motive whatever, in that particular case. But the common sense of twelve honest men gives still a better chance of just decision than the hazard of cross and pile.

—*Notes on the State of Virginia*, 1782

The care of every man's soul belongs to himself. But what if he neglect[s] the care of it? Well what if he neglect[s] the care of his health or estate . . . ? Will the magistrate make a law that he shall not be poor or sick? Law provide against injury from others, but not from ourselves. God himself will not save men against their wills.

—Notes labeled "Scraps Early in the Revolution," October 1776

A strict observance of the written laws is doubtless one of the high duties of a good citizen, but it is not the highest. The laws of necessity, of self-preservation, of saving our country when in danger, are of higher obligations. To lose our country by a scrupulous adherence to written law would be to lose the law itself, with life, liberty, property and all those who are enjoying them with us; thus absurdly sacrificing the end to the means.

—Letter to John B. Colvin, September 20, 1810

Law is quite overdone. It is fallen to the ground, and a man must have great powers to raise himself in it to either honor or profit. The mob of the profession get as little money and less respect than they would by digging the earth. The physician is happy in the attachment of the families in which he practices. If, to the consciousness of having saved some lives, he can add that of having, at no time, from want of caution, destroyed the boon he was called to save, he will enjoy, in age, the happy reflection of not having lived in vain, while the lawyer has only to recollect how many, by his dexterity, have been cheated of their right and reduced to beggary.

—Letter to Judge David Campbell, January 28, 1810

RELIGION, MORALITY, AND VIRTUE

Fix reason firmly in her seat, and call to her tribunal every fact, every opinion. Question with boldness even the existence of a god; because, if there be one, he must more approve of the homage of reason, than that of blindfolded fear.

—Letter to Peter Carr, August 10, 1787

We are not in a world ungoverned by the laws and power of a superior agent. Our efforts are in his hand and directed by it; and he will give them their effect in his own time.

—Letter to David Barrow, May 1, 1815

I never told my own religion, nor scrutinized that of another. I never attempted to make a convert, nor wished to change another's creed. I have ever judged of the religion of others by their lives. . . . For it is in our lives, and not from our words, that our religion must be read.

—Letter to Margaret Bayard Smith, August 6, 1816

It does me no injury for my neighbor to say there are twenty Gods, or no God.

—*Notes on the State of Virginia, 1782*

No man complains of his neighbor for ill management of his affairs, for an error in sowing his land, or marrying his daughter, for consuming his substance in taverns . . . in all these he has liberty; but if he does not frequent the church, or then conform in ceremonies, there is an immediate uproar.

—*Notes on the State of Virginia, 1782*

Believing with you that religion is a matter which lies solely between man and his God, that he owes account to none other for faith or his worship, that the legislative powers of government reach actions only, and not opinions, I contemplate with solemn reverence that act of the whole American people which declared that their legislature should "make no law respecting an establishment of religion, or prohibiting the free exercise thereof," thus building a wall of separation between Church and State.

—*Letter to the Danbury Baptists, January 1, 1802*

Of all the systems of morality, ancient or modern, which have come under my observation, none appear to me so pure as that of Jesus.

—*Letter to William Canby, September 18, 1813*

Had the doctrines of Jesus been preached always as purely as they came from his lips, the whole civilised world would now have been Christian.

—Letter to Benjamin Waterhouse, June 26, 1822

I consider the doctrines of Jesus as delivered by himself to contain the outlines of the sublimest system of morality that has ever been taught but I hold in the most profound detestation and execration the corruptions of it which have been invented . . . .

—Letter to Henry Fry, June 17, 1804

Among the sayings and discourses imputed to [Jesus] by his biographers, I find many passages of fine imagination, correct morality, and of the most lovely benevolence; and others again of so much ignorance, so much absurdity, so much untruth, charlatanism, and imposture, as to pronounce it impossible that such contradictions should have proceeded from the same being. I separate, therefore, the gold from the dross; restore to Him the former, and leave the latter to the stupidity of some, and roguery of others of His disciples. Of this band of dupes and impostors, Paul was the great Coryphaeus, and first corruptor of the doctrines of Jesus. These palpable interpolations and falsifications of His doctrines, led me to try to sift them apart.

—Letter to William Short, April 13, 1820

No historical fact is better established, than that the doctrine of one God, pure and uncompounded, was that of the early ages of Christianity... Nor was the unity of the Supreme Being ousted from the Christian creed by the force of reason, but by the sword of civil government, wielded at the will of the fanatic Athanasius. The hocus-pocus phantasm of a God like another Cerberus, with one body and three heads, had its birth and growth in the blood of thousands of martyrs... The Athanasian paradox that one is three, and three but one, is so incomprehensible to the human mind, that no candid man can say he has any idea of it, and how can he believe what presents no idea? He who thinks he does, only deceives himself. He proves, also, that man, once surrendering his reason, has no remaining guard against absurdities the most monstrous, and like a ship without rudder, is the sport of every wind. With such person, gullibility which they call faith, takes the helm from the hand of reason, and the mind becomes a wreck.

—Letter to James Smith, December 8, 1822

The priests of the different religious sects, who dread the advance of science as witches do the approach of day-light; and scowl on it the fatal harbinger announcing the subversion of the duperies on which they live. In this the Presbyterian clergy take the lead. the tocsin is sounded in all their pulpits, and the first alarm denounced is against the particular creed of Doctr. Cooper; and as impudently denounced as if they really knew what it is.

—Letter to José Francesco Corrê a Da Serra, April 11, 1820

Nay, we have heard it said that there is not a Quaker or a Baptist, a Presbyterian or an Episcopalian, a Catholic or a Protestant in heaven; that on entering that gate, we leave those badges of schism behind...Let us not be uneasy about the different roads we may pursue, as believing them the shortest, to that our last abode; but following the guidance of a good conscience, let us be happy in the hope that by these different paths we shall all meet in the end. And that you and I may meet and embrace, is my earnest prayer. And with this assurance I salute you with brotherly esteem and respect.

—Letter to Miles King, September 26, 1814

The moral sense, or conscience, is as much a part of man as his leg or arm. It is given to all human beings in a stronger or weaker degree, as force of members is given them in a greater or less degree. It may be strengthened by exercise, as may any particular limb of the body. This sense is submitted, indeed, in some degree, to the guidance of reason; but it is a small stock which is required for this: even a less one than what we call common sense. State a moral case to a ploughman and a professor. The former will decide it as well, and often better than the latter, because he has not been led astray by artificial rules.

—Letter to Peter Carr, August 10, 1787

I view great cities as pestilential to the morals, the health and the liberties of man. True, they nourish some of the elegant arts, but the useful ones can thrive elsewhere, and less perfection in the others, with more health, virtue and freedom, would be my choice.

—Letter to Benjamin Rush, September 23, 1800

We are firmly convinced . . . that with nations, as with individuals, our interests soundly calculated, will ever be found inseparable from our moral duties.

—Second Inaugural Address, March 4, 1805

Reading, reflection and time have convinced me that the interests of society require the observation of those moral precepts only in which all religions agree, for all forbid us to steal, murder, plunder or bear false witness.

—Letter to James Fishback, September 27, 1809

The moral sense is as much a part of our constitution as that of feeling, seeing, or hearing.

—Letter to John Adams, October 14, 1816

Morality, compassion, generosity are innate elements of the human constitution.

—Letter to Pierre-Samuel Du Pont, April 24, 1816

Whenever you are to do a thing, though it can never be known but to yourself, ask yourself how you would act were the whole world looking at you, and act accordingly.

—Letter to Peter Carr, August 19, 1785

Give up money, give up fame, give up science, give the earth itself and all it contains, rather than do an immoral act.

—Letter to Peter Carr, August 19, 1785

My principle is to do whatever is right, and leave consequences to Him who has the disposal of them.

—Letter to George Logan, September 20, 1813

He who permits himself to tell a lie once, finds it much easier to do it a second and third time, till at length it becomes habitual; he tells lies without attending to it, and truths without the world's believing him. This falsehood of the tongue leads to that of the heart, and in time depraves all its good dispositions.

—Letter to Peter Carr, August 19, 1785

Truth will do well enough if left to shift for herself. She seldom has received much aid from the power of great men to whom she is rarely known & seldom welcome. She has no need of force to procure entrance into the minds of men. Error indeed has often prevailed by the assistance of power or force. Truth is the proper & sufficient antagonist to error.

—*Notes on Religion*, October 1776

I . . . never believed there was one code of morality for a public [man], and another for a private man.

—Letter to Don Valentine de Feronda, October 4, 1809

There is not a truth existing which I fear, or would wish unknown to the whole world.

—Letter to Henry Lee, May 15, 1826

The man who fears no truths has nothing to fear from lies.

—Letter to George Logan, 1816

Men are disposed to live honestly, if the means of doing so are open to them.

—Letter to François de Marbois, June 14, 1817

Those who labor in the earth are the chosen people of God, if ever he had a chosen people, whose breasts he has made his peculiar deposit for substantial and genuine virtue. It is the focus in which he keeps alive that sacred fire, which otherwise might escape from the face of the earth.

—*Notes on the State of Virginia,* 1782

Peace, War, and the Military

It is time enough for the rightful purposes of civil government for its officers to interfere when principles break out into overt acts against peace and good order.

—The Virginia Act for Religious Freedom, 1786

Peace and friendship with all mankind is our wisest policy, and I wish we may be permitted to pursue it.

—Letter to Charles William Frederick Dumas, May 6, 1786

Justice indeed, on our part, will save us from those wars which would have been produced by a contrary disposition. But how can we prevent those produced by the wrongs of other nations? By putting ourselves in a condition to punish them. Weakness provokes insult and injury, while a condition to punish, often prevents them.

—Letter to John Jay, August 23, 1785

I love peace, and I am anxious that we should give the world
still another useful lesson, by showing to them other modes of
punishing injuries than by war, which is as much a punishment to
the punisher as to the sufferer.

—Letter to Tench Coxe, May 1, 1794

War is an instrument entirely inefficient toward redressing wrong;
and multiplies, instead of indemnifying losses.

—Letter to John Sinclair, 1798

In times of peace the people look most to their representatives; but
in war, to the executive solely.

—Letter to Caesar A. Rodney, February 10, 1810

I have seen enough of one war never to wish to see another.

—Letter to John Adams, April 25, 1794

Whensoever hostile aggressions . . . require a resort to war, we must
meet our duty and convince the world that we are just friends and
brave enemies.

—Letter to Andrew Jackson, December 3, 1806

The spirit of this country is totally adverse to a large military force.

—Letter to Chandler Price, February 28, 1807

For a people who are free, and who mean to remain so, a well-organized and armed militia is their best security.

—Message to Congress, November 8, 1808

Every citizen [should] be a soldier. This was the case with the Greeks and the Romans, and must be that of every free state.

—Letter to James Monroe, 1813

POLITICS AND PATRIOTISM

You and I have formerly seen warm debates and high political passions. But gentlemen of different politics would then speak to each other and separate the business of the Senate from that of society. It is not so now. Men who have been intimate all their lives, cross the streets to avoid meeting, and turn their heads another way, lest they should be obliged to touch their hats. This may do for young men with whom passion is enjoyment. But it is afflicting to peaceable minds. Tranquility is the old man's milk.

—Letter to Edward Rutledge, June 24, 1797

Politics are such a torment that I would advise every one that I love not to mix with them.

—Letter to Martha Jefferson Randolph, February 11, 1800

Politics, like religion, hold up the torches of martyrdom to the reformers of error.

—Letter to James Ogilvie, August 4, 1811

If I could not go to heaven but with a party, I would not go there at all.

—Letter to Francis Hopkinson, March 13, 1789

Men by their constitutions are naturally divided into two parties: 1. Those who fear and distrust the people, and wish to draw all powers from them into the hands of the higher classes. 2. Those who identify themselves with the people, have confidence in them, cherish and consider them as the most honest and safe, although not the most wise depository of the public interests. . . . Call then. . .Whigs and Tories, Republicans and Federalists, Aristocrats and Democrats, or by whatever name you please, they are the same parties still, and pursue the same object.

—Letter to Henry Lee, August 10, 1824

Where the private interests of a member are concerned in a bill or question, he is to withdraw. And where such an interest has appeared, his voice has been disallowed, even after a division. In a case so contrary not only to the laws of decency, but to the fundamental principle of the social compact, which denies to any man to be a judge in his own cause, it is for the honor of the House that this rule, of immemorial observance, should be strictly adhered to.

—*A Manual of Parliamentary Practice*, 1801

When a man assumes a public trust, he should consider himself as public property.

—Jefferson's remark to Baron von Humboldt,
quoted in *Life of Jefferson*, by B. L. Raynor

If a due participation of office is a matter of right, how are vacancies to be obtained? Those by death are few; by resignation none.

—Letter to E. Shipman, July 12, 1801

Whenever a man has cast a longing eye on offices, a rottenness begins in his conduct.

—Letter to Tench Coxe, 1799

Be a listener only, keep within yourself, and endeavor to establish with yourself the habit of silence, especially on politics. In the fevered state of our country, no good can ever result from any attempt to set one of these fiery zealots to rights, either in fact or principle. They are determined as to the facts they will believe, and the opinions on which they will act. Get by them, therefore, as you would by an angry bull; it is not for a man of sense to dispute the road with such an animal.

—Letter to Thomas Jefferson Randolph, November 24, 1808

If the present Congress errs in too much talking, how can it be otherwise in a body to which the people send 150 lawyers, whose trade it is to question everything, yield nothing, and talk by the hour? That 150 lawyers should do business together ought not to be expected.

—Jefferson's *Autobiography*

My affections were first for my own country, and then, generally, for all mankind.

—Letter to Thomas Law, January 15, 1811

The patriot, like the Christian, must learn that to bear revilings & persecutions is a part of his duty; and in proportion as the trial is severe, firmness under it becomes more requisite & praiseworthy.

—Letter to James Sullivan, May 21, 1805

The Presidency

His character was, in its mass, perfect, in nothing bad, in few points indifferent; and it may truly be said that never did nature and fortune combine more perfectly to make a man great.

—Jefferson's remark about George Washington in
letter to Dr. Walter Jones, January 2, 1814

My first wish is a restoration of our just rights; my second, a return of the happy period, when, consistently with duty, I May withdraw myself totally from the public stage and pass the rest of my days in domestic ease and tranquillity, banishing every desire of ever hearing what passes in the world.

—Letter to John Randolph, 1775

You hope I have not abandoned entirely the service of our country. After five and twenty years' continual employment in it, I trust it will be thought I have fulfilled my tour, like a punctual soldier, and May claim my discharge. But I am glad of the sentiment from you, because it gives a hope you will practice what you preach, and come forward in aid of the public vessel. I will not admit your old excuse that you are in public service though at home. The campaigns which are fought in a man's own house are not to be counted. The present situation of the President, unable to get the offices filled, really calls with uncommon obligation on those whom nature has fitted for them.

—Letter to Edward Rutledge, 1795

I have no ambition to govern men. It is a painful and thankless office.

—Letter to John Adams, December 28, 1796

I know well that no man will ever bring out of that office the reputation which carries him into it. The honeymoon would be as short in that case as in any other, and its moments of ecstasy would be ransomed by years of torment and hatred.

—Letter to Edward Rutledge, December 27, 1796

As to Mr. Adams, particularly, I could have no feelings which would revolt at being placed in a secondary station to him. I am his junior in life, was his junior in Congress, his junior in the diplomatic line, his junior lately in the civil government.

—Letter to James Madison, 1797

I sincerely wish we could see our government so secured as to depend less on the character of the person in whose hands it is trusted. Bad men will sometimes get in, and with such an immense patronage, May make great progress in corrupting the public mind and principles. This is a subject with which wisdom and patriotism should be occupied.

—Letter to George Gilmer, 1787

The little spice of ambition which I had in my younger days has long since evaporated, and I set still less store by a posthumous than present name.

—Letter to James Madison, 1795

The second office of the government is honorable and easy, the first is but a splendid misery.

—Letter to Elbridge Gerry, 1797

Called upon to undertake the duties of the first executive office of our country, I avail myself of the presence of that portion of my fellow citizens which is here assembled, to express my grateful thanks for the favor with which they have been pleased to look toward me, to declare a sincere consciousness that the task is above my talents, and that I approach it with those anxious and awful presentiments which the greatness of the charge and the weakness of my powers so justly inspire. A rising nation, spread over a wide and fruitful land, traversing all the seas with the rich productions of their industry, engaged in commerce with nations who feel power and forget right, advancing rapidly to destinies beyond the reach of mortal eye—when I contemplate these transcendent objects, and see the honor, the happiness, and the hopes of this beloved country, I shrink from the contemplation, and humble myself before the magnitude of the undertaking.

—First Inaugural Address, March 4, 1801

Peace, commerce, and honest friendship with all nations, entangling alliances with none.

—First Inaugural Address, March 4, 1801

Disapproving myself of transferring the honors and veneration for the great birthday of our Republic to any individual, or of dividing them with individuals, I have declined my own birthday be known, and have engaged my family not to communicate it. This has been the uniform answer to every application of the kind.

—Letter to Levi Lincoln, August 1803

The only birthday which I recognize is that of my country's liberties.

—*The Life of Thomas Jefferson* by B. L. Rayner

The acquisition of New Orleans would of itself have been a great thing, as it would have ensured to our western brethren the means of exporting their produce; but that of Louisiana is inappreciable, because, giving us the sole dominion of the Mississippi, it excludes those bickerings with foreign powers, which we know of a certainty would have put us at war with France immediately; and it secures to us the course of a peaceful nation.

—Letter to John Dickinson, August 1803

The acquisition of Louisiana, although more immediately beneficial to the western States, by securing for their produce a certain market, not subject to interruptions by officers over whom we have no control, yet is also deeply interesting to the maritime portion of our country, inasmuch as by giving the exclusive navigation of the Mississippi, it avoids the burthens and sufferings of a war, which conflicting interests on that river would inevitably have produced at no distant period. It opens, too, a fertile region for the future establishments in the progress of that multiplication so rapidly taking place in all parts.

—Message to the Tennessee Legislature, 1803

The territory acquired, as it includes all the waters of the Missouri and Mississippi, has more than doubled the area of the United States, and the new part is not inferior to the old in soil, climate, productions and important communications.

—Letter to General Horatio Gates, 1803

On this important acquisition, so favorable to the immediate interests of our western citizens, so auspicious to the peace and security of the nation in general, which adds to our country territories so extensive and fertile, and to our citizens new brethren to partake of the blessings of freedom and self government, I offer to Congress and the country, my sincere congratulations.

—Special Message to Congress, January 1804

I sincerely regret that the unbounded calumnies of the federal party have obliged me to throw myself on the verdict of my country for trial, my great desire having been to retire, at the end of the present term, to a life of tranquillity; and it was my decided purpose when I entered into office. They force my continuance. If we can keep the vessel of State as steadily in her course for another four years, my earthly purposes will be accomplished, and I shall be free to enjoy. . . my family, my farm, and my books.

—Letter to Elbridge Gerry, 1804

The danger is that the indulgence and attachments of the people will keep a man in the chair after he becomes a dotard. . . . General Washington set the example of voluntary retirement after eight years. I shall follow it. And a few more precedents will oppose the obstacle of habit to any one after awhile who shall endeavor to extend his term.

—Letter to John Taylor, January 6, 1805

The expedition of Messrs. Lewis and Clark, for exploring the river Missouri, and the best communication from that to the Pacific ocean, has had all the success which could have been expected. They have traced the Missouri nearly to its source, descended the Columbia to the Pacific ocean, ascertained with accuracy the geography of that interesting communication across our continent, learned the character of the country, of its commerce, and inhabitants; and it is but justice to say that Messrs. Lewis and Clark, and their brave companions, have by this arduous service deserved well of their country.

—Sixth Annual Message to Congress, December 1806

The greatest favor which can be done me is the communication of the opinions of judicious men, of men who do not suffer their judgments to be biased by either interests or passions.

—Letter to Chandler Price, 1807

I confess that I am not reconciled to the idea of a chief magistrate parading himself through the several States, as an object of public gaze, and in quest of an applause which, to be valuable, should be purely voluntary. I had rather acquire silent good-will by a faithful discharge of my duties, than owe expressions of it to my putting myself in the way of receiving them.

—Letter to James Sullivan, 1807

I am tired of an office where I can do no more good than many others, who would be glad to be employed in it. To myself, personally, it brings nothing but unceasing drudgery and daily loss of friends. Every office becoming vacant, every appointment made, *me donne un ingrat, et cent ennemis.* My only consolation is in the belief that my fellow citizens at large will give me credit for good intentions.

—Letter to John Dickinson, 1807

Within a few days I retire to my family, my books, and farms; and having gained the harbor myself, I shall look on my friends still buffeting the storm with anxiety indeed, but not with envy. Never did a prisoner released from his chains feel such relief as I shall on shaking off the shackles of power. Nature intended me for the tranquil pursuits of science by rendering them my supreme delight. But the enormities of the times in which I have lived have forced me to take a part in resisting them and to commit myself on the boisterous ocean of political passions. I thank God for the opportunity of retiring from them without censure and carrying with me the most consoling proofs of public approbation. I leave everything in the hands of men so able to take care of them, that if we are destined to meet misfortunes, it will be because no human wisdom could avert them.

—Letter to P. S. Dupont de Nemours, March 2, 1809

The pomp, the turmoil, the bustle and splendor of office, have drawn but deeper sighs for the tranquil and irresponsible occupations of private life.

—Letter to Inhabitants of Albemarle County, April 3, 1809

FAMILY, FRIENDS, AND HOME

My father's education had been quite neglected, but, being of a strong mind, sound judgment and eager after information, he read much and improved himself.

—Jefferson's *Autobiography*

He was the third or fourth settler of the part of the country in which I live, which was about 1737. He died Aug. 17, 1757, leaving my mother a widow who lived till 1776, with six daughters & two sons, myself the elder.

—Jefferson's *Autobiography*

Jane Jefferson
Ah Jane, best of girls!
Flower snatched away in its bloom!
May the earth weigh lightly upon you!
Farewell for a long, long time

—Jefferson's epitaph for his favorite sister, Jane, who died at the age of 25,
from *Thomas Jefferson: A Life* by Willard Sterne Randall

Offer prayers for me, too, at that shrine to which, tho' absent, I pay continual devotion. In every scheme of [my] happiness, she is placed in the foreground of the picture, as the principal figure. Take that away, and it is no picture for me.

—Letter to R. Skipwith, writing about Martha Wayles Skelton,
during their courtship, August 3, 1773

For god's sake, for your country's sake and for my sake, come. I receive by every post such accounts of the state of Mrs. Jefferson's health that it will be impossible for me to disappoint her expectation of seeing me at the time I have promised. . . . I pray you to come. I am under a sacred obligation to go home.

—Letter to Richard Henry Lee, July 29, 1776, wherein Jefferson
implores Lee to relieve him of his responsibilities in Philadelphia
so he may attend to his wife who suffered bouts of severe depression

I expect that you will write to me by every post. Inform me what books you read, what tunes you learn, and inclose me your best copy of every lesson in drawing . . . Take care that you never spell a word wrong . . . I have placed my happiness on seeing you good and accomplished, and no distress which this world can now bring on me could equal that of your disappointing my hopes. If you love me then, strive to be good under every situation.

—Jefferson's letter to his eleven-year-old daughter, Martha (Patsy)
in 1783, from *Understanding Thomas Jefferson* by E. M. Halliday

Time wastes too fast: every letter
I trace tells me with what rapidity
life follows my pen. The days and hours
of it are flying over our heads like
clouds of a windy day never to return—
more. Every thing presses on—and every
time I kiss thy hand to bid adieu, every absence which
follows it, are preludes to that eternal separation
which we are shortly to make!

—Laurence Sterne's *Tristram Shandy,* which Thomas Jefferson and his dying wife
Martha copied together before her death in September of 1782. Jefferson kept the
paper inside a private cabinet in his bedroom until his death in 1826

Your letter found me a little emerging from the stupor of mind
which had rendered me as dead to the world as she whose loss
occasioned it. . . . Before that event my scheme of life had been
determined. I had folded myself in the arms of retirement, and
rested all prospects of future happiness on domestic and literary
objects. A single event wiped away all my plans and left me a
blank which I had not the spirits to fill up. In this state of mind
an appointment from Congress found me, requiring me to cross
the Atlantic.

—Letter to Chevalier de Chastellux, November 1782, about the death of his wife

I find as I grow older, that I love those most whom I loved first.

—Letter to Mrs. John Bolling, 1787

Ten years of unchequered happiness.

—Jefferson's words describing his marriage to "Patty," quoted in
Jefferson: A Great American's Life and Ideas by Saul K. Padover

When languishing under disease, how grateful is the solace of
our friends! How are we penetrated with their assiduities and
attentions! How much are we supported by their encouragement
and kind offices! When heaven has taken from us some object of
our love, how sweet is it to have a bosom whereon to recline our
heads, and into which we may pour the torrent of our tears! Grief,
with such a comfort, is almost a luxury!

—Letter to Mrs. Maria Cosway, October 12, 1786

Heart. And what more sublime delight than to mingle tears with
one whom the hand of heaven hath smitten! To watch over the
bed of sickness & to beguile it's tedious & it's painful moments! To
share our bread with one to whom misfortune left none! This world
abounds indeed with misery: to lighten its burthen we must divide
it with one another.

—Letter to Mrs. Maria Cosway, October 12, 1786

The happiness of your life depends now on the continuing to please
a single person. To this all other subjects must be secondary; even
your love to me. . . .

—Letter to Martha Jefferson just before her marriage, 1790

I had rather be shut up in a very modest cottage with my books, my family and a few old friends, dining on simple bacon, and letting the world roll on as it liked, than to occupy the most splendid post, which any human power can give.

—Letter to Alexander Donald, February 7, 1788

The happiest moments of my life have been the few which I have passed at home in the bosom of my family.

—Letter to Francis Willis, Jr., 1790

Every human being must thus be viewed, according to what it is good for; for none of us, no not one, is perfect; and were we to love none who had imperfections, this world would be a desert for our love. All we can do is to make the best of our friends, love and cherish what is good in them, and keep out of the way of what is bad; but no more think of rejecting them for it, than of throwing away a piece of music for a flat passage or two. Your situation will require peculiar attentions and respect to both parties. Let no proof be too much for either your patience or acquiescence. Be you the link of love, union, and peace for the whole family. The world will give you the more credit for it, in proportion to the difficulty of the task, and your own happiness will be the greater as you perceive that you promote that of others.

—Letter to Martha Jefferson Randolph, 1790, wherein Jefferson advises his daughter on how to get along with her father-in-law's new young wife

The one [letter] announced that you were become a notable house-wife, the other a mother. This last is undoubtedly the key-stone of the arch of matrimonial happiness, as the first is it's daily aliment.

—Letter to Martha Jefferson Randolph, February 9, 1791

Harmony in the marriage state is the very first object to be aimed at.

—Letter to Mary (Polly) Jefferson Eppes, January 7, 1798

These reveries . . . leave me always impressed with the desire of being at home once more, and of exchanging labour, envy, and malice, for the ease, domestic occupation, and domestic love and society, where I may once more be happy with you, and Mr. Randolph, and dear little Anne, with whom even Socrates might ride on a stick without being ridiculous.

—Letter to Martha Jefferson Randolph, January 15, 1792

The motion of my blood no longer keeps time with the tumult of the world. It leads me to seek for happiness in the lap and love of my family, in the society of my neighbors and my books, in the wholesome occupations of my farm and my affairs, in an interest or affection in every bud that opens, in every breath that blows around me, in an entire freedom of rest, of motion, of thought, owing account to myself alone of my hours and actions.

—Letter to James Madison, 1793

Tranquility is the old man's milk. I go to enjoy it in a few days, and to exchange the roar and tumult of bulls and bears for the prattle of my grandchildren and senile rest.

—Letter to Edward Rutledge, June 24, 1797

The circle of our nearest connections is the only one in which faithful and lasting affection can be found, one which will adhere to us under all changes and chances. It is therefore the only soil on which it is worth while to bestow much culture.

—Letter to Mary Jefferson Eppes, January 1, 1799

Environed here [Philadelphia] in scenes of constant torment, malice and obloquy, worn down in a station where no effort to render service can aver any thing, I feel not that existence is a blessing but when something recalls my mind to my family or farm. This was the effect of your letter, and its affectionate expressions kindled up all those feelings of love for you and our dear connections which now constitute the only real happiness of my life.

—Letter to Martha Jefferson Randolph, February 7, 1799

It is in the love of one's family only that heartfelt happiness is known.

—Letter to Mary Jefferson Eppes, 1801

Others may lose of their abundance, but I, of my want, have lost even the half of what I had. My evening prospects hang on the slender thread of a single life. Perhaps I may be destined to see even this last cord of parental affection broken! The hope with which I had looked forward to the moment when, resigning public cares to younger hands, I was to retire to that domestic comfort from which the last great step is to be taken, is fearfully blighted.

—Letter to John Page, June 25, 1804, in which Jefferson expresses his grief over the death of his daughter Mary (Polly) and reveals his fear that his daughter Martha would likewise be taken from him

I never consider a difference of opinion in politics, in religion, in philosophy, as cause for withdrawing from a friend.

—The Life and Writings of Thomas Jefferson edited by Samuel E. Forman

No apologies for writing or speaking to me freely are necessary. On the contrary, nothing my friends can do is so dear to me, and proves to me their friendship so clearly, as the information they give me of their sentiments and those of others on interesting points where I am to act, and where information and warning are so essential to excite in me that due reflection which ought to precede action.

—Letter to Wilson C. Nicholas, 1803

When you and I look out on the country over which we have passed, what a field of slaughter does it exhibit. Where are all the friends who entered it with us, under all the inspiring energies of health and hope? As if pursued by the havoc of war, they are strewed by the way, some earlier, some later, and scarce a few straglers remain to count the numbers fallen, and to mark yet by their own fall the last footsteps of their party.

—Letter to John Page, June 25, 1804

Mr. Adams's friendship and mine began at an early date. It accompanied us through long and important scenes. The different conclusions we had drawn from our political reading and reflections, were not permitted to lessen personal esteem; each party being conscious they were the result of an honest conviction in the other. Like differences of opinion existing among our fellow citizens, attached them to one or the other of us, and produced a rivalship in their minds which did not exist in ours. We never stood in one another's way; for if either had been withdrawn at any time, his favorers would not have gone over to the other, but would have sought for some one of homogeneous opinions. This consideration was sufficient to keep down all jealousy between us, and to guard our friendship from any disturbance by sentiments of rivalship.

—Letter to Abigail Adams, June 1804

Mr. Adams has been alienated from me, by belief in the lying suggestions contrived for electioneering purposes, that I perhaps mixed in the activity and intrigues of the occasion. My most intimate friends can testify that I was perfectly passive. They would sometimes, indeed, tell me what was going on; but no man ever heard me take part in such conversations; and none ever misrepresented Mr. Adams in my presence, without my asserting his just character. With very confidential persons I have doubtless disapproved of the principles and practices of his administration. This was unavoidable. But never with those with whom it could do him any injury. Decency would have required this conduct from me, if disposition had not, and I am satisfied Mr. Adams's conduct was equally honorable towards me. But I think it part of his character to suspect foul play in those of whom he is jealous, and not easily to relinquish his suspicions.

—Letter to Benjamin Rush, 1811

Nothing new has happened in our neighborhood since you left us. The houses and trees stand where they did. The flowers come forth like the belles of the day, have their short reign of beauty and splendor, and retire like them to the more interesting office of reproducing their like. The hyacinths and tulips are off the stage, the Irises are giving place to the Belladonnas, as this will to the Tuberoses &c. As your Mamma has done to you, my dear Anne, as you will do to the sisters of little John, and I shall soon and chearfully do to you all in wishing you a long, long, goodnight.

—Letter to his granddaughter, Anne Cary Randolph Bankhead, May 1811

Our grandfather read our hearts to see our invisible wishes.

> —Ellen W. Coolidge, Jefferson's granddaughter, 1850,
> from *The Domestic Life of Thomas Jefferson* by Sarah Randolph

A letter from you calls up recollections very dear to my mind.
It carries me back to the to the times when, beset with difficulties
and dangers, we were fellow laborers in the same cause, struggling
with what is most valuable to man, his right of self-government.
Laboring always at the same oar, with some wave ever ahead
threatening to overwhelm us and yet passing under our bark, we
knew not how, we rode through the storm with heart and hand,
and made a happy port.

> —Letter to John Adams, January 21, 1812, sent in response to a note from Adams.
> The two had not spoken for twelve years after their bitterly waged presidential
> election of 1800. With this letter, their friendship was renewed and they shared a rich
> correspondence until their deaths, within hours of one another, on July 4, 1826.

There is no degree of affliction, produced by the loss of those
dear to us, which experience has not taught me to estimate.
I have ever found time and silence the only medicine, and these
but assuage, they never can suppress, the deep drawn sigh which
recollection forever brings up, until recollection and life are
extinguished together.

> —Letter to John Adams 1813

I see no comfort in outliving one's friends, and remaining a mere monument of the times which are past.

—Thomas Jefferson, letter to Charles Pinckney, September 3, 1816

Tried myself in the school of affliction, by the loss of every form of connection which can rive the human heart, I know well, and feel what you have lost, what you have suffered, are suffering, and have yet to endure. The same trials have taught me that for ills so immeasurable, time and silence are the only medicines. I will not, therefore, by useless condolences, open afresh the sluices of your grief, nor, although mingling sincerely my tears with yours, will I say a word more where words are vain.

—Letter to John Adams, where Jefferson offers condolences to his friend on the death of Abigail Adams, November 13, 1818

For after one's friends are all gone before them, and our faculties leaving us too, one by one, why wish to linger in mere vegetation, as a solitary trunk in a desolate field, from which all it's former companions have disappeared.

—Letter to Mrs. Maria Cosway, December 27, 1820

And our own dear Monticello, where has nature spread so rich a mantle under the eye? mountains, forests, rocks, rivers. With what majesty do we there ride above the storms! How sublime to look down into the workhouse of nature, to see her clouds, hail, snow, rain, thunder, all fabricated at our feet! And the glorious Sun, when rising as if out of a distant water, just gilding the tops of the mountains, and giving life to all nature!

—Letter to Mrs. Maria Cosway, October 12, 1786

I have nothing interesting to tell you from hence but that we are well, and how much we love you. From Monticello you have every thing to write about which I have any care. How do my young chestnut trees? How comes on your garden? How fare the fruit blossoms etc.

—Letter to Martha Jefferson Randolph, March 24, 1793

All my wishes end, where I hope my days will end, at Monticello. Too many scenes of happiness mingle themselves with all the recollections of my native woods and fields, to suffer them to be supplanted in my affection by any other.

—Letter to George Gilmer, 1787

Books, the Arts, and Life's Pleasures

The loss of my mother's house by fire, and in it, of every paper I had in the world, and almost every book. On a reasonable estimate I calculate the cost of the books burned to have been £200 sterling. Would to god it had been the money; then had it never cost me a sigh!

—Letter to John Page, 1770

I cannot live without books.

—Letter to John Adams, June 10, 1815

Misery is often the parent of the most affecting touches in poetry.

—*Notes on the State of Virginia*, 1782

A little attention however to the nature of the human mind evinces that the entertainments of fiction are useful as well as pleasant. That they are pleasant when well written every person feels who reads. But wherein is its utility asks the reverend sage, big with the notion that nothing can be useful but the learned lumber of Greek and Roman reading with which his head is stored? I answer, everything is useful which contributes to fix in the principles and practices of virtue.

—Letter to Robert Skipwith, August 3, 1771

Some of the most agreeable moments of my life have been spent in reading works of imagination which have this advantage over history that the incidents of the former may be dressed in the most interesting form, while those of the latter must be confined to fact. They cannot therefore present virtue in the best and vice in the worst forms possible, as the former may.

—Letter to Charles Brockden Brown, January 15, 1800

A lively and lasting sense of filial duty is more effectually impressed on the mind of a son or daughter by reading *King Lear*, than by all the dry volumes of ethics, and divinity, that ever were written.

—Letter to Robert Skipwith, August 3, 1771

We never reflect whether the story we read be truth or fiction. If the painting be lively, and a tolerable picture of nature, we are thrown into a reverie, from which if we awaken it is the fault of the writer. I appeal to every reader of feeling and sentiment whether the fictitious murder of Duncan by Macbeth in Shakespeare does not excite in him as great a horror of villainy as the real one of Henry IV by Ravaillac as related by Davila? And whether the fidelity of Nelson and generosity of Blandford in Marmontel do not dilate his breast and elevate his sentiments as much as any similar incident which real history can furnish? Does he not, in fact, feel himself a better man while reading them, and privately covenant to copy the fair example?

—Letter to Robert Skipwith, August 3, 1771

A great obstacle to good education is the inordinate passion prevalent for novels, and the time lost in that reading which should be instructively employed. When this poison infects the mind, it destroys its tone and revolts it against wholesome reading. . . . This mass of trash, however, is not without some distinction; some few modelling their narratives, although fictitious, on the incidents of real life, have been able to make them interesting and useful vehicles of sound morality. . . . For a like reason, too, much poetry should not be indulged. Some is useful for forming style and taste. Pope, Dryden, Thompson, Shakespeare, and of the French, Molière, Racine, the Corneilles, may be read with pleasure and improvement.

—Letter to Nathaniel Burwell, March 14, 1818

I have often thought that nothing would do more extensive good at small expense than the establishment of a small circulating library in every county, to consist of a few well-chosen books, to be lent to

the people of the country under regulations as would secure their
safe return in due time.

—Letter to John Wyche, May 19, 1809

I have given up newspapers in exchange for Tacitus and Thucydides,
for Newton and Euclid; and I find myself much the happier.

—Letter to John Adams, January 21, 1812

I feel a much greater interest in knowing what has passed two
or three thousand years ago, than in what is now passing. I read
nothing, therefore, but of the heroes of Troy, of the wars of
Lacedaemon and Athens, of Pompey and Caesar, and of Augustus
too, the Bonaparte and parricide scoundrel of that day.... I slumber
without fear, and review in my dreams the visions of antiquity.

—Letter to Nathaniel Macon, January 12, 1819

My greatest of all amusements, reading.

—Letter to Abigail Adams, August 22, 1813

If you visit me as a farmer, it must be as a co-disciple; for I am but
a learner; an eager one indeed, but yet desperate, being too old now
to learn a new art. However, I am as much delighted and occupied
with it, as if I was the greatest adept. I shall talk with you about it

from morning till night, and put you on very short allowance as to political aliment. Now and then a pious ejaculation for the French and Dutch republicans, returning with due dispatch to clover, potatoes, wheat, &c.

—Letter to W. B. Giles, 1795

I am an enthusiast on the subject of the arts. But it is an enthusiasm of which I am not ashamed, as its object is to improve the taste of my countrymen, to increase their reputation, to reconcile to them the respect of the world, and procure them its praise.

—Letter to James Madison, 1785

Do not neglect your music, it will be a companion which will sweeten many hours of life to you.

—Letter to Martha Jefferson Randolph, April 4, 1790

No occupation is so delightful to me as the culture of the earth, & no culture comparable to that of the garden. but tho' an old man, I am but a young gardener.

—Letter to Charles Willson Peale, August 20, 1811

When I contemplate the immense advances in science, and discoveries in the arts which have been made within the period of

my life, I look forward with confidence to equal advances by the
present generation; and have no doubt they will consequently be
as much wiser than we have been, as we than our fathers were, and
they than the burners of witches.

—Letter to Benjamin Waterhouse, March 3, 1818

Nature intended me for the tranquill pursuits of science, by
rendering them my supreme delight. but the enormities of the
times in which I have lived, have forced me to take a part in
resisting them, and to commit myself on the boisterous ocean
of political passions.

—Letter to Pierre Samuel Du Pont de Nemours, March 2, 1809

You know my collection, its condition and extent. I have been fifty
years making it, and have spared no pains, opportunity or expense,
to make it what it is. While residing in Paris, I devoted every
afternoon I was disengaged, for a summer or two, in examining all
the principal book stores, turning over every book with my own
hand, and putting by everything which related to America, and
indeed whatever was rare and valuable in every science. Besides
this, I had standing orders during the whole time I was in Europe,
on its principal book-marts, particularly Amsterdam, Frankfort,
Madrid and London, for such works relating to America as could
not be found in Paris. So that in that department particularly, such
a collection was made as probably can never again be effected,

because it is hardly probable that the same opportunities, the same time, industry, perseverance and expense, with some knowledge of the bibliography of the subject, would again happen to be in concurrence. During the same period, and after my return to America, I was led to procure, also, whatever related to the duties of those in the high concerns of the nation. So that the collection, which I suppose is of between nine and ten thousand volumes, while it includes what is chiefly valuable in science and literature generally, extends more particularly to whatever belongs to the American Statesman. In the diplomatic and parliamentary branches, it is particularly full.

—Letter to S. H. Smith, September 1814, on the sale
of his library to the Library of Congress

Good wine is a necessity of life for me.

—*The Man from Monticello: An Intimate Life of Thomas Jefferson*
by Thomas J. Fleming

Wisdom of
Thomas Jefferson

Perfect happiness I believe was never intended by the deity to be the lot of any one of his creatures. . . . The most fortunate of us, in our journey through life, frequently meet with calamities and misfortunes which may greatly afflict us; and, to fortify our minds against the attacks of these calamities and misfortunes should be one of the principal studies and endeavors of our lives. The only method of doing this is to assume a perfect resignation to the Divine will, to consider that whatever does happen, must happen; and that, by our uneasiness, we cannot prevent the blow before it does fall, but we may add to its force after it has fallen. These considerations, and others such as these, may enable us in some measure to surmount the difficulties thrown in our way; to bear up with a tolerable degree of patience under the burden of life; and to proceed with a pious and unshaken resignation, till we arrive at our journey's end, when we may deliver up our trust into the hands of Him who gave it, and receive such reward as to him shall seem proportioned to our merit.

—Letter to John Page, July 15, 1763

An honest heart being the first blessing, a knowing head is the second.

—Letter to Peter Carr, August 19, 1785

Take more pleasure in giving what is best to another than in having it yourself, and then all the world will love you, and I more than all the world.

—Letter to his daughter, Mary Jefferson, April 11, 1790

Conscience is as much a part of man as his leg or arm. It is given to all human beings in a stronger or weaker degree . . . It may be strengthened by exercise . . . Therefore, read good books, as they will encourage as well as direct your feelings.

—Letter to Peter Carr, August 10, 1787

Your affectionate mother requests that I would address to you, as a namesake, something which might have a favorable influence on the course of the life you have to run. Few words are necessary with good dispositions on your part. Adore God. Reverence and cherish your parents. Love your neighbor as yourself; and your country more than life. Be just. Be true. Murmur not at the ways of providence and the life into which you have entered will be a passage to one of eternal and ineffable bliss. And if to the dead it is permitted to care for the things of this world, every action of your life will be under my regard.

—Letter to Thomas Jefferson Grotjan, January 10, 1824

A Decalogue of Canons for observation in practical life

Never put off till tomorrow what you can do today.

Never trouble another for what you can do yourself.

Never spend your money before you have it.

Never buy what you do not want, because it is cheap;
    it will be dear to you.

Pride costs us more than hunger, thirst, and cold.

We never repent of having eaten too little.

Nothing is troublesome that we do willingly.

How much pain have cost us the evils which have
    never happened.

Take things always by their smooth handle.

When angry, count to ten, before you speak; if very
    angry, an hundred.

—Letter to Thomas Jefferson Smith, February 21, 1825. Also included
in Benjamin Franklin's Poor Richard's Almanack.

[I have never] been able to conceive how any rational being
could propose happiness to himself form the exercise of power
over others.

—Letter to Destutt de Tracy, January 26, 1811

An honest man can feel no pleasure in the exercise of power over
his fellow citizens.

—Letter to John Melish, January 13, 1813

Neither believe nor reject anything because any other persons or description of persons have rejected or believed it. Your own reason is the only oracle given you by heaven.

—Letter to Peter Carr, August 10, 1787

It was one of the rules which, above all, made Doctor Franklin the most amiable of men in society, "never to contradict anybody." If he was urged to announce an opinion, he did it rather by asking questions, as if for information, or by suggesting doubts. When I hear another express an opinion which is not mine, I say to myself, he has a right to his opinion, as I to mine; why should I question it? His error does me no injury.

—Letter to Thomas Jefferson Randolph, November 24, 1808

In truth, politeness is artificial good humor, it covers the natural want of it, and ends by rendering habitual a substitute nearly equivalent to the real virtue. It is the practice of sacrificing to those whom we meet in society, all the little inconveniences and preferences which will gratify them, and deprive us of nothing worth a moment's consideration; it is the giving a pleasing and flattering turn to our expressions, which will conciliate others, and make them pleased with us as well as themselves. How cheap a price for the good will of another!

—Letter to Thomas Jefferson Randolph, November 24, 1808

Give about two [hours], every day, to exercise; for health must not be sacrificed to learning. A strong body makes the mind strong.

—Letter to Peter Carr, August 19, 1785

The sovereign invigorator of the body is exercise, and of all exercises, walking is best.

—Letter to Thomas Mann Randolph, Jr., August 27, 1786

Games played with the ball, and others of that nature, are too violent for the body, and stamp no character on the mind.

—Letter to Peter Carr, August 19, 1785

Take care that you never spell a word wrong. Always before you write a word, consider how it is spelled, and, if you do not remember it, turn to a dictionary. It produces great praise to a lady to spell well.

—Letter to his daughter, Martha Jefferson, 1783

It is while we are young that the habit of industry is formed. If not then, it never is afterwards. The fortune of our lives, therefore, depends on employing well the short period of youth.

—Letter to his daughter, Martha Jefferson, March 28, 1787

Delay is preferable to error.

—Letter to George Washington, May 16, 1792

A mind always employed is always happy. This is the true secret, the grand recipe for felicity. The idle are the only wretched. In a world which furnishes so many emploiments which are useful, and so many which are amusing, it is our own fault if we ever know what ennui is.

—Letter to his daughter, Martha Jefferson, May 21, 1787

I never submitted the whole system of my opinions to the creed of any party of men whatever in religion, in philosophy, in politics, or in anything else where I was capable of thinking for myself. Such an addiction is the last degradation of a free and moral agent.

—Letter to Francis Hopkinson, March 13, 1789

HIS FINAL YEARS

I have withdrawn myself from all political intermeddlings, to
indulge the evening of my life with what have been the passions
of every portion of it, books, science, my farms, my family and
friends. To these every hour of the day is now devoted.

—Letter to James Maury, April 25, 1812

The hand of age is upon me. All my old friends are nearly gone.
Of those in my neighborhood, Mr. Divers and Mr. Lindsay alone
remain. If you could make it a *partie quarrée,* it would be a comfort
indeed. We would beguile our lingering hours with talking over
our youthful exploits, our hunts on Peter's mountain, with a long
train of et cetera, in addition, and feel, by recollection at least,
a momentary flash of youth. Reviewing the course of a long
and sufficiently successful life, I find in no portion of it happier
moments than those were.

—Letter to James Maury, April 25, 1812

As to federal slanders, I never wished them to be answered but by
the tenor of my life, half a century of which has been on a theatre
at which the public have been spectators, and competent judges of
its merit. Their approbation has taught a lesson, useful to the world,
that the man who fears no truths has nothing to fear from lies.
I should have fancied myself half guilty had I condescended to put
pen to paper in refutation of their falsehoods, or drawn to them
respect by any notice from myself.

—Letter to George Logan, 1816

There is a ripeness of time for death regarding others as well as
ourselves, when it is reasonable we should drop off, and make room
for another growth. I am happy in what is around me. Yet I assure
you I am ripe for leaving all, this year, this day, this hour.

—Letter to John Adams, August 1, 1816

This keeps me at the drudgery of the writing-table all the prime
hours of the day, leaving for the gratification of my appetite for
reading, only what I can steal from the hours of sleep. Could
I reduce this epistolary corvée within the limits of my friends
and affairs, and give the time redeemed from it to reading and
reflection, to history, ethics, mathematics, my life would be as happy
as the infirmities of age would admit.

—Letter to Charles Thomson, January 8, 1816

The earth belongs to the living, not to the dead.

—Letter to John W. Eppes, June 24, 1813

I was a hard student until I entered on the business of life, the duties of which leave no idle time to those disposed to fulfil them; and now, retired, and at the age of seventy-six, I am again a hard student. Indeed, my fondness for reading and study revolts me from the drudgery of letter writing. . . . I am not so regular in my sleep as the Doctor says he was, devoting to it from five to eight hours, according as my company or the book I am reading interests me; and I never go to bed without an hour, or half hour's previous reading of something moral, whereon to ruminate in the intervals of sleep.

—Letter to Vine Utley, March 21, 1819

My business is to beguile the wearisomeness of declining life, as I endeavor to do, by the delights of classical reading and of mathematical truths, and by the consolations of a sound philosophy, equally indifferent to hope and fear.

—Letter to William Short, October 31, 1819

A system of general instruction, which shall reach every description of our citizens, from the richest to the poorest, as it was the earliest, so will it be the latest, of all the public concerns in which I shall permit myself to take an interest.

—Letter to Joseph C. Cabell, January 14, 1818

This institution [University of Virginia] will be based on the illimitable freedom of the human mind. for here we are not afraid to follow truth wherever it may lead, nor to tolerate any error so long as reason is left free to combat it.

—Letter to William Roscoe, December 27, 1820

I have generally great aversion to the insertion of my letters in the public papers; because of my passion for quiet retirement, and never to be exhibited in scenes on the public stage.

—Letter to John Adams, 1822

My spirits have never failed me except under those paroxysms of grief which you, as well as myself, have experienced in every form: and with good health and good spirits the pleasures surely outweigh the pains of life. Why not then taste them again, fat and lean together.

—Letter to John Adams, December 18, 1825

I know that I turned to neither book nor pamphlet while writing it. I did not consider it as any part of my charge to invent new ideas altogether, and to offer no sentiments which had never been expressed before . . . I pray God that these principles may be eternal, and close the prayer with my affectionate wishes for yourself of long life, health and happiness.

—Letter to James Madison, where Jefferson recalls writing
the Declaration of Independence, August 30, 1823

A death-bed Adieu. Th:J to MR.
Life's visions are vanished, it's dreams are no more.
Dear friends of the bosom, why bathed in tears?
I go to my fathers; I welcome the shore,
which crowns all my hopes, or which buries my cares.
Then farewell my dear, my lov'd daughter, Adieu!
The last pang in life is in parting from you!
Two Seraphs await me, long shrouded in death:
I will bear them your love on my last parting breath.

—Jefferson's poem to his daughter, Martha Jefferson Randolph,
written several days before his death on July 4, 1826

All eyes are opened, or opening, to the rights of man. The general spread of the light of science has already laid open to every view the palpable truth, that the mass of mankind has not been born with saddles on their backs, nor a favored few booted and spurred, ready to ride them legitimately, by the grace of God. These are grounds of hope for others. For ourselves, let the annual return of this day forever refresh our recollections of these rights, and an undiminished devotion to them.

—Letter to Roger C. Weightman, wherein Jefferson declines to attend the ceremonies in Washington D.C. celebrating the fiftieth anniversary of Independence due to his failing health. Written June 24, 1826, this was Jefferson's last letter.

This is the Fourth?

—Jefferson's last words. He died on July 4, 1826, the 50th anniversary of the signing of the Declaration of Independence.

Here was buried
Thomas Jefferson
Author of the Declaration of American Independence
of the Statute of Virginia for religious freedom
and Father of the University of Virginia.

—Jefferson's Epitaph, written by himself, and inscribed on his tombstone

Remembrances of
Thomas Jefferson

His mind must have been by nature one of uncommon
capaciousness and retention, of wonderful clearness and as rapid
as is consistent with accurate thoughts. His application from
early youth [was] not only intense but unremitted. When young,
he adopted a system, perhaps an entire plan of life from which
neither the exigencies of business nor the allurements of pleasure
could drive or seduce him. Much of his success is to be ascribed to
methodical industry.

—Francis Walker Gilmer, contemporary of Jefferson, from
Thomas Jefferson: A Life by Willard Sterne Randall

He pursued the law with an eager industry. . . . Reserved toward
the world at large, to his intimate friends he shewed a peculiar
sweetness of temper and by them was admired and beloved. . . .
He panted after the fine arts and discovered a taste in them not
easily satisfied with such scanty means as existed in a colony. . . . It
constituted a part of Mr. Jefferson's pride to run before the times in
which he lived. [He was] an admirer of elegance and convenience.

—Edmund Randolph, one of Jefferson's lawyer colleagues, from
Thomas Jefferson: A Life by Willard Sterne Randall

Mr. Jefferson came into Congress, in June, 1775, and brought with him a reputation for literature, science, and a happy talent of composition. Writings of his were handed about, remarkable for the peculiar felicity of expression. Though a silent member in Congress, he was so prompt, frank, explicit, and decisive upon committees and in conversation, not even Samuel Adams was more so, that he soon seized upon my heart. . . .

—John Adams, letter to Thomas Pickering, 1822

Mr. Jefferson is one of the most amiable, learned, upright and able men who ever existed.

—Marquis de Lafayette

Let me describe you a man, not yet forty, tall, and with a mild and pleasing countenance, but whose mind and understanding are ample substitutes for every exterior grace. An American, who without ever having quitted his own country, is at once a musician, skilled in drawing, a geometrician, an astronomer, a natural philosopher, legislator, and statesman. . . . I found his first appearance serious, nay even cold; but before I had been two hours with him we were as intimate as if we had passed our whole lives together; walking, books, but above all, a conversation always varied and interesting.

—Marquis de Chastellux, French aristocrat visiting Monticello in 1782, from *Jefferson: A Great American's Life and Ideas* by Saul K. Padover

He thinks by this step to get a reputation as a humble, modest, meek man, wholly without ambition or vanity. He may have deceived himself into this belief. But if the prospect opens, the world will see and he will feel that he is as ambitious as Oliver Cromwell.

—John Adams, 1793, commenting on Jefferson's proposed "retirement"

By God, he had rather be on his farm than to be made emperor of the world.

—Attributed to George Washington, speaking of Thomas Jefferson

Your character as a philosopher and friend of mankind predominates so much more in my mind over that of your new station.... You have opened a new era.

—Benjamin Rush, letter to Thomas Jefferson upon Jefferson's first inauguration, March 12, 1801

In conversation he is free and communicative. All topics that fall under discussion are treated by him with equal unreservedness. He seems, indeed, to have no thought or opinion to conceal and his store of knowledge are unlocked and laid open with the same freedom in which nature unfolds her bounties. They lie before you, and you have only to select and enjoy.... The liberality of his disposition, is felt in blessings around the neighbourhood of Monticello.

—Joseph Delaplaine, 1815, close friend of Jefferson's who established the first national portrait gallery

I consider you and him as the North and South Poles of the American Revolution. Some talked, some wrote, and some fought to promote and establish it, but you and Mr. Jefferson thought for us all.

—Benjamin Rush to John Adams, referring to
Adams and Jefferson, February 17, 1812

The principles of Jefferson are the axioms of a free society.

—Abraham Lincoln

All to honor Jefferson—to the man who, in the concrete pressure of a struggle for national independence by a single people, had the coolness, forecast, and capacity to introduce into a merely revolutionary document, an abstract truth, and so to embalm it there, that to-day, and in all coming days, it shall be a rebuke and a stumbling block to the very harbingers of re-appearing tyranny and oppression.

—Abraham Lincoln, letter to H. L. Pierce and others, April 6, 1859

I think this is the most extraordinary collection of talent, of human knowledge, that has ever been gathered together at the White House with the possible exception of when Thomas Jefferson dined alone.

—John F. Kennedy, remarked at dinner honoring Nobel Prize
winners of the Western Hemisphere, April 29, 1962

No man in this or any other country in the Western world—
excepting only Leonardo da Vinci—ever matched Jefferson in the
range of his activities, in the fertility of his thinking, and in the
multiplicity of his interests. The number of things Jefferson did, or
knew how to do, still astonishes. He was a mathematician, surveyor,
architect, paleontologist, prosodist, lawyer, philosopher, farmer,
fiddler and inventor. He set up an educational system; he built a
university; he founded a great political party; he helped design
the national capital; he was instrumental in establishing America's
coinage; he doubled the territory of the United States; he invented
machines and gadgets; he collected scientific material in the fields
of zoology, geology and anthropology; he wrote a classic essay on
poetry; he codified the legal system of his native State. Everything
interested him; nothing was alien to his mind.

—Saul K. Padover from *Jefferson: A Great American's Life and Ideas*

The contradictions in Jefferson's character have always rendered it a
fascinating study.

. . . Almost every other American statesman might be described
in a parenthesis. A few broad strokes of the brush would paint
the portraits of all the early Presidents with this exception, and
a few more strokes would answer for any member of their many
cabinets; but Jefferson could be painted only touch by touch, with
a fine pencil, and the perfection of the likeness depended upon the
shifting and uncertain flicker of its semi-transparent shadows.

—Henry Brooks Adams from *History of the United States of America during the
Administrations of Thomas Jefferson and James Madison*

Jefferson was a man in motion. It was no accident that he was a superb horseman. He was at ease with philosophes, but he was not at his best in cool contemplation. He had his finest ideas and achieved his finest expression of them in the crucible of controversy. His mind worked best when he had to respond to crisis or rise to a rhetorical occasion. He was in his element looking to the future, ill at ease looking at the past.

—Michael Zuckerman's introduction to *The Autobiography of Thomas Jefferson*, 2005 edition

He did embody, outstandingly and consistently, very much of what we mean when we think of the word "American" as something to be proud of and thankful for. He did, in his two terms as president, set the country on the course that has made it the greatest representative democracy in this troubled world, potentially the best hope of mankind for a good, free, and happy life.

—E. M. Halliday from *Understanding Thomas Jefferson*

CHRONOLOGY OF
THOMAS JEFFERSON

April 2 [or 13] 1743 — Born at Shadwell in Albemarle County, Virginia.

1757 — Jefferson's father, Peter Jefferson, dies.

1760 — Attends William and Mary College.

1762 — Graduates from William and Mary College.

1762 — Studies law with George Wythe at Williamsburg.

1767 — Admitted to practice law from Shadwell.

1768 — Elected to House of Burgesses.

1770 — Begins construction at Monticello.

1772 — Marries Martha Wayles Skelton, daughter Martha born.

1774 — Writes "A Summary View of the Rights of British America." Jefferson retires from the practice of law. At his father-in-law's death, he inherits 11,000 acres of land and 135 slaves. His daughter, Jane, is born.

1775 — Elected to Continental Congress. Daughter Jane dies.

1776 — Drafted Declaration of Independence. Elected to Virginia House of Delegates and is appointed to revise Virginia laws. Mother Jane Randolph Jefferson dies.

1777 — Drafts Virginia Statute for Religious Freedom, which is passed in 1786 by the General Assembly. A son is born and dies.

1778 — Third daughter, Mary Jefferson, is born.

1779 to 1781 — Serves as Governor of Virginia.

1780 — Daughter Lucy Elizabeth born. Begins writing *Notes on the State of Virginia.*

1781 — Lucy Elizabeth dies.

1782 — Second child named Lucy Elizabeth is born. Several months after the birth of this baby, wife Martha dies.

1783 — Elected delegate to Congress.

1784 to 1789 — Elected Commissioner and Minister to France. Completes Notes on the State of Virginia. Daughter Lucy Elizabeth dies.

1790 to 1793 — Serves as first U.S. Secretary of State.

1797 to 1801 — Serves as U.S. Vice President.

1801 to 1809 — Serves as U.S. President

1803 — Louisiana Purchase concluded. Lewis and Clark expedition is launched.

1804 — Daughter Mary Jefferson Eppes dies at the age of 25. Jefferson is left with one surviving member of his immediate family, his daughter Martha, who would outlive Jefferson and become the mother of eleven living children.

1809 — Retires from presidency and public life. Continues to remodel Monticello.

1815 — With debts pressing in on him, Jefferson sells his 6,500-volume library to Congress after the British burned the Library of Congress in 1814.

1825 — University of Virginia is opened.

1826 — Jefferson dies at Monticello on July 4, five hours before the death of John Adams.